A Small Map of Experience

Reflections & Aphorisms

ESSENTIAL TRANSLATIONS SERIES 8

We acknowledge the financial support
of the Government of Canada through
the Canada Book Fund (CBF) for our publishing activities.

LEONIDAS DONSKIS

A Small Map of Experience

Reflections & Aphorisms

TRANSLATED FROM THE LITHUANIAN
by
KARLA GRUODIS

GUERNICA
TORONTO • BUFFALO • BERKELEY • LANCASTER (U.K.)
2013

Michael Mirolla, editor
David Moratto, book designer
Guernica Editions Inc.
P.O. Box 117, Station P, Toronto (ON), Canada M5S 2S6
2250 Military Road, Tonawanda, N.Y. 14150-6000 U.S.A.

Distributors:
University of Toronto Press Distribution,
5201 Dufferin Street, Toronto (ON), Canada M3H 5T8
Gazelle Book Services, White Cross Mills, High Town,
Lancaster LA1 4XS U.K.

First edition.
Printed in Canada.

Legal Deposit – Third Quarter
Library of Congress Catalog Card Number: 2012941657
Library and Archives Canada Cataloguing in Publication

Donskis, Leonidas
A small map of experience :
reflections and aphorisms / Leonidas
Donskis ; Karla Gruodis, translator.

(Essential translations series ; 8)
Translation of: Mažasis patirties žemėlapis:
mintys ir aforizmai.
Issued also in electronic format.
ISBN 978-1-55071-660-3

1. Aphorisms and apothegms. I. Gruodis, Karla II. Title. III.
Series: Essential translations series (Toronto, Ont.) ; 8

PN6277.L5D66 2012   891'.9284   C2012-904227-7

Foreword

———✦———

AN APHORISM IS a distilled, laconic reflection about the author's intimate experiences of reality, expressed through paradox, provocation, or shocking self-disclosure. Aphorisms cannot be conceived theoretically, and one cannot learn how to write them from a manual. They rise up out of authentic experience — from silence and pauses, from stopping oneself so that a thought is not drowned by the flood of words and pretentious expressions. A person who speaks too much is unlikely to succeed in writing aphorisms or maxims. When writing about things that one has experienced and grasped directly, rather than learned from some theoretical or academic lesson, economy of thought and language are key.

From childhood I have been an ardent admirer of such thinkers as Marcus Aurelius, de la Rochefoucauld, Pascal, and Poincaré, and have long thought about writing a book of reflections, maxims, and aphorisms.

Here are some of my favourite winged phrases:

> *Even if it's not true, it's well conceived.*
> (Italian proverb)

> *The best revenge is to be unlike him who performed the injury.* (Marcus Aurelius)

> *To doubt everything, or to believe everything, are two equally convenient solutions; both dispense with the necessity of reflection.* (Henri Poincaré)

> *We all have enough strength to endure the misfortunes of others.*
> (François de la Rochefoucauld)

An aphorism is also a space for dialogue: it is an open and unfinished thought, which always requires that we, as readers, go back and attempt to develop the ellipses and silences which the author has left for us like an invitation. The aphorism is, in essence, a form of fragmentary writing, so it is not surprising that it has been popular with modern and postmodern thinkers such as Lichtenberg, Schopenhauer, Nietzsche, Wittgenstein and Baudrillard. Like a jazz improvisation, it does not give the author any chance to hide, or to conceal anything. It is a confession — an idea expressed as much through its form as its content.

In this book, dear reader, you will find not only aphorisms, but fragments of thoughts, each of which could be expanded into a book chapter or an article. Deliberately left unfinished, they are like aphorisms because they invite the reader to return to them.

This kind of book has been best described by Jean Baudrillard:

> Fragmentary writing is, ultimately, democratic writing. Each fragment enjoys an equal distinction. Even the most banal finds its exceptional

reader. Each, in turn, has its hour
of glory. Of course, each fragment
could become a book. But the point is
that it will not do so, for the ellipsis
is superior to the straight line ...

— JEAN BAUDRILLARD, *Fragments:
Cool Memories III, 1990–1995*

And so this book fulfils my old dream of
offering my thoughts and aphorisms to the
English reader, thus giving my more
intimate and less academic work a second
life. Two people made this happen. For
invaluable advice, guidance into the world
of non-academic writing and publishing,
and unflagging support, I owe a huge debt
of gratitude to Antanas Sileika. For her
most sensitive and masterful translation of
my book, and her magic touch as a native
speaker of both Lithuanian and English, I
am immensely grateful to Karla Gruodis.

For her generosity, kindness, and sup-
port, my warm thanks are also due to
Mrs. Birutė Garbaravičienė, Chair of the
Editorial Board of the publishing group
SC Baltic Media.

— LEONIDAS DONSKIS

My Dinner with Leonidas

———◆◆◆———

Academic, philosopher, Euro-parliamentarian, Leonidas Donskis is also an excellent dinner table companion, with whom I have shared hasty, yet exquisite meals in a variety of settings from hotel dining rooms to the terrace outside his home in a former czarist army barrack. One dines with him for the conversations, whose subjects can range from models for Eastern European revival to moral standards in a globalizing world to musings on the writings of Arthur Koestler to the best songs of the Beatles (which he might play on the piano or guitar) to the recipe for lamb shanks *en papillote* to his understanding of himself as a child of Holocaust survivors. The talk is intense, with humorous asides, and often seeks insight into the heart of matters both big and small, and I always leave the table wondering about the nature of life and fate and society in a way I had not before the meal.

This collection of aphorisms reads like snatches from those dinner conversations with the bridges (and the recipes and music) eliminated, leaving compressed insights that bear further thought.

On the one hand, the insights ask us to wonder about timeless questions, such as how to achieve happiness (not by seizing the world, but adapting to it), and on the other hand the aphorisms address contemporary concerns such as the impact of globalization (an expression of failed hope).

At times the vocabulary sounds like something straight out of the period of Marcus Aurelius, terms such as *wisdom* and *nobility*, and at others like that of a cultural critic reacting to the childish speech in today's new generations (which have extended adolescence and immaturity).

Insight mixes with irony and occasional melancholy (it is unappealing to return to the city where one was born) and the problem of being a Jew and of talking about Jews.

There is nothing quite like a dinner with Leonidas, often in the company of his wife, Jolanta. But this collection of reflections and aphorisms is like a series of notes from those meals — the notes themselves are fascinating, and they open the doors to subjects which merit further investigation.

— ANTANAS SILEIKA

1

AN APHORISM IS that which remains
after a painful battle with the excesses
of one's own language and experience.

2

THERE IS NO such thing as being alone,
because we can always see and listen
to the world. Loneliness amongst others
only prevents us from understanding
the world and ourselves.

3

INTENSITY OF THOUGHT and spirit
are a function of one's grasp of,
and reconciliation with, the brief
time in which one lives.

4

IF WE SERIOUSLY engage in the games
of power, our success or failure are but
masks of fate or freedom which in turn
conceal mechanisms of social control.

5

SEVERITY IS BUT a mask for pedagogical
righteousness that in turn conceals
impulses of power and social control.

6

GIVEN THE CHOICE to relive some
of life's moments, most of us choose
those of joy and happiness, even though
they are meaningless without those
of sadness and loss.

7

WHAT IS WISDOM? It is the ability to see
the face of every person one speaks to,
to hear everything they say.

8

WHAT IS NOBILITY? It is the courage
and ability to see as good and wise not
only those who like and are like us.

9

WHAT IS HAPPINESS? It is the ability to
reconcile one's character with the world,
and in particular with those one loves.

10

WHAT IS A spectacular career? It is
a deliriously fast transition from living
in the present to planning life in terms
of months and years.

11

TRUE INDIVIDUAL FREEDOM is usually
expressed as courtesy and respect
for others — not only out of fear,
but from the knowledge that one
is limited and flawed.

12

THERE IS AN aspect of genius within
those who recognize it.

13

SOME ARTISTS ARE perfect products
of their age, while others actively help
to create it. These are two aspects of the
same social dynamic: either one reflects
one's time or becomes an alternative
to it. Each is equally important
to the social and political thinker.

14

A WISE THOUGHT is often built on the
foundation of two contradictory follies.

15

EXCESSIVE CRITICISM IS often nothing but
the ability to feed off of another's
talent — to make oneself the centre of
attention by opposing someone superior.

16

IN CHOOSING VENGEANCE one can claim
to be reducing the number of bad and
dangerous people in the world, but
by choosing their methods one is only
increasing their number by one.

17

IN THE MALE imagination, a beautiful
piece of woman's clothing is the shortest
path to an appreciation of her body.

18

GOODNESS, BEAUTY, AND truth never
call themselves by these names; they
allow us to see, hear, and understand
the world without dividing it into
opposing categories.

19

AESTHETIC MATURITY MEANS confronting
the original works in whose
reproductions one delighted as a youth.

20

THE CULT OF celebrity stems from
an inability to feel reality. Only in
England can cooks become pop culture
icons — something that would
be unimaginable in Italy. One only has
to think of the many chefs, much better
than Jamie Oliver, who are working
quietly away in small Italian village
restaurants. It would never occur
to Italy's Olivieri that they could
be TV stars. In their country chefs only
become famous by starting a social or
cultural movement like Giacomo Maioli's
Slow Food. Italians don't need media
wizardry to make up for a lack
of real experience.

21

AN INDIVIDUALIST BELIEVES that one enters the world alone and leaves it alone. Everything else — success, relations with others, memory — is but a fragile human treasure that means nothing either to the newly born or to the dying. One is thrust into this reality naked and alone, and that is how one leaves it. The traditionalist would say the opposite: that without the participation of others we can neither be born nor appropriately depart from this world. In terms of world views, the first is clearly closer to liberalism, the second to conservatism. In terms of form and movement of thought, the first looks more like a philosopher or a writer, the second like a sociologist or anthropologist. Just as the style of thought and writing one chooses shapes one's language, so does language inspire the content of thought. Paradoxically, both groups are right.

22

IN THE END, we love that which
we cannot rationally explain, but without
which we would not be able to integrate
our self and our identity into a unified
whole. We love that which we are afraid
to lose, and which, without us, would
lose its being. We cannot love that which
exists or will continue to exist without
us. We love when the logic of the heart
whispers that this is the only way
to distil one's self and to find
meaning in existence.

23

INTELLIGENT MIND AND bodily
intelligence — these are two different
realities. Even talented actors or athletes
have difficulty expressing themselves
through language, and are unable
to exploit its possibilities. On the other
hand, thinkers and skilled orators often
do not know what to do with their
bodies, especially their hands. They
usually don't like to dance and can't

see the beauty in sport. Their own
bodies are not intelligent.

24

BUREAUCRATIC INSTITUTIONS IN the
practice of demeaning people often
favour sentimental décor. Once, while
spending a few hours at an airport,
I found myself in a US Immigration and
Naturalization office — an establishment
that can prevent people from entering
the country for no clear reason, ask
humiliating questions, and send them
off without explanation. The children's
drawings decorating its walls send the
world a message about America's purity
and idealism. Many years later I saw
a similar thing in a tax inspector's office
in my own country. Although an
oppressive place, it too was decorated
with children's drawings. Are they
trying to remind us that, when we
enter such places, we all become
children in need of care and control?
Or are they exposing their fantasies
of social manipulation?

25

EXCESSIVE SEVERITY OFTEN masks
the fear that, by acting in a friendly
and forgiving way, one might appear
silly and weak.

26

THOSE WHO SPEAK publicly and eagerly
about their faith are often those who use
it as a tool for controlling the thoughts
and behaviour of others.

27

JUST AS EXCESSIVE talk about sexuality
betrays the speaker's hidden problems
in this area, excessive talk about religion
reveals a desperate need to overcome
one's own lack of faith — while
simultaneously masking one's frustration
with, and even hatred for, peaceful
and authentic believers and non-believers.

28

ACCORDING TO THE classical formula
of power, you can see me only when you
merit it or have transgressed, because
allowing you to see me is an act of grace
or punishment. According to the modern
formula of power, I can see you as much
as and whenever I want to, but you do
not have the same right to see me.
According to the postmodern formula
of power, I will force you to see me
the way you are obliged to, and only
when necessary; you will not see me
when you want to, and certainly not
as you would like to.

29

PEOPLE ONLY KNOW that which they
are not afraid to know. They understand
only that which they truly want
to understand, and do not understand
that which they actively try not to.
This is perfectly expressed in English
as "the will to misunderstand."

30

PHILOSOPHERS OFTEN JUMP straight from youthful immaturity, poorly concealed by theoretical and linguistic masks, to misanthropic, geriatric irritability, often failing to achieve wisdom in the process.

31

LIFE IS A slow leap from the child's dislike of adults to the senior's dislike of all humanity.

32

ONE'S HOMELAND IS the only place in the world where one can experience true self-love and true self-hatred — often at the same time.

33

PUBLIC SPACE IS nothing but the translation of influential people's private lives into public concerns.

34

SUCCESS ACCORDING TO today's popular culture: a long youth marked by pubertal or post-pubertal traits such as childish speech and the puerile desire to please those in power (that is, adults), while sometimes safely rebelling against them; dispassionate sex with myriad partners, who are treated like consumer goods that need to be sampled for true satisfaction to be achieved; hysterical public reactions to the results of contests and competitions, and so on. A calm and quiet person, one who pauses while speaking, will never be able to join this celebration of extended adolescence and immaturity. To get invited one must smile constantly and, when receiving a major prize, shed meaningful tears and thank one's family — that is, the metaphorical family of loving producers and other power brokers who created that success.

35

SUCCESS IS NEVER final and misfortune
never fatal. And if occasionally something
doesn't work out — not something
imposed on us by the entertainment
industry, but something we did
ourselves — we are left a bit more wise
and mature. We may, of course, feel sad,
but that only reinforces our faith in the
meaningfulness of our work and choices.

36

LIFE IS LIKE playing the piano:
we only draw out its deepest,
most authentic sounds when our time
on Earth is coming to an end.

37

SHOULD SOMEONE'S AGE be a factor
in a discussion? Not really, because one
can always remain blind and deaf to life's
lessons. Wisdom and nobility are not
necessarily related to or dependent

on age. The older master's willingness
to bow to the abilities of a protégé
is not only indicative of their shared code
of ethics and behaviour, but also of their
recognition that they both bow to a third,
higher party, such as God, conscience,
or a moral principle. Submission to that
which gives us meaning and allows
us to be ourselves is the truest
manifestation that we value life.

38

LIFE OFTEN SLIPS away just as we are
getting ready to start living. But is there
any way to prepare for it? That would be
the same as trying to plan how one will
think and speak during the course
of a conversation. There are no special
or worthless periods in one's life — only
the unifying effort to understand the
nature of existence, and that is impossible
without imagination and dreaming.
We must be able to feel immortal for
at least a heartbeat if we are to dare
to dream, to think, and to be ourselves.

39

ONE LOVES THAT which one is afraid
to lose and does passionately that which
can be interrupted at any time.

40

MUSIC TEACHERS SOMETIMES tell their
students to play as though they are giving
their last performance, because only
then will people be able to hear and
trust them. But if a musician plays
in one performance while thinking
about a later one, neither effort will
be successful. It is the same with life.
One must live knowing that it can
be broken off at any time, and that
there just might not be time, later,
to recognize and correct one's errors.

41

WE ARE BUT a footstep between the flash
of life's passage and immortal hope.

42

PEACE IS A coward's dream only
according to pre-modern political
and moral thought. To achieve peace, we
must overcome our natural impulse
to avenge ourselves or our loved
ones — an impulse that modern
civilization has more or less managed
to inhibit through the rule of law. That
is why the strong and the wise long
for peace. It inspires them to create
a higher social and moral order — to
direct their greatest strengths toward
the creation and improvement of life
rather than allow them to be wasted
on war and destruction.

43

WHILE FORCE EXISTS only in its external
manifestations, power permeates every
layer of civilization. The difference
between force and power is the
difference between the armed criminal

or warrior's aggressive demeanour and
that of his well-dressed master, who can
order his subjects with a smile and
a look. It is the difference between
a gunshot and the handkerchief that
signals that the trigger be pulled.

44

EVEN THOUGH IT is tempting to agree
with the logical assertion that
remorseless scoundrels should
be liquidated, the danger will always
remain that, through acts of revenge
and violence, their number will
be increased rather than reduced.

45

IT IS SOMETIMES mistakenly thought that
villainy is the product of ignoble goals.
But we have all at some point considered
criminal acts or, speaking for myself, at
least fantasized about that which we
would not really want to do. True villainy
is the use of all means, no matter how
contemptible, to achieve our goals. But to

annihilate our enemies we must do things
that will destroy us too, that will drown
us in a torrent of aggression. By entering
the realm of force we are trapped by its
operating logic — the need to protect
ourselves and the fear of revenge.

46

FRUSTRATION IS USUALLY caused
by a lack of self-awareness. We let
upsetting and destructive experiences
eat away at us, rationalizing them into
ideas about the imperfection, perversion,
and hostility of the world. If, instead
of examining ourselves, we blame
our surroundings for all our ills,
we will never find peace.

47

TALK LESS ABOUT yourself and take more
interest in the lives of others. As you
come to know them and understand how
they speak, you will begin to understand
yourself. If you use others as a screen
on which to project your own social

and psychological drama, you will fail
to know either them or yourself.

48

WE SOMETIMES THINK that power
corrupts slowly and gradually, but that
is not true — it corrupts instantly.
At first, though, the newly powerful
might still remain attuned to their
surroundings, careful not to speak
naturally or to reveal their personal
truths and values.

49

I HAVE THE urge to modify Lord Acton's
otherwise perfect aphorism: "Power
reveals, and absolute power reveals
absolutely." Psychologists and sociologists
tell us that sudden changes in a person's
life can significantly alter his or her
personality — the resistance fighter
becomes a dictator; the just and
honourable person stops consulting with
close friends and becomes dependent on

a handful of plotters and sycophants; the
leader with noble pursuits becomes blind
to friends and family and starts blaming
these quietly suffering people rather than
seeing that his or her failures are the
result of dangerous and ambitious goals.

50

DOES POWER CORRUPT even the noble?
It probably does, except in the rare cases
of those who can maintain a good sense
of humour and resolve not to take
themselves too seriously. It can be
tempting to confuse power with virtue,
strength with truth. Power invariably
rips a person from what I would call his
or her natural social environment; unlike
partnerships and collegial relations,
it produces an asymmetry of strength
that deforms even close friendships
unless people consciously detach
themselves from its field. If you represent
an institution or a whole country,
the danger lurks that, even when
mistaken, you will identify with that body

and fail to understand that it is you, and only you, who is being criticized — not your country, your nation, or its history.

51

ARE THERE ANY situations in which power does not corrupt? Perhaps, but only when a person who has gained power acts like a doctor or teacher after hours — after all, these professionals do not subject their family and friends to operations or lectures. One must avoid surrendering to the field of power. If one does not maintain a conscious, relative relationship with one's self, one risks losing one's humanity and becoming a caricature — a living monument that speaks not to people, but to history and eternity. Let us not be taken hostage by power's imagination.

52

LIKE ABSOLUTE POWER, the logic of war equates force and truth.

53

Variation on George Orwell.

ACCORDING TO THE logic of the
twentieth century, wars were historically
won by those who were left standing.
The wars of the future will be different.
No one will really win them or have
the goal of winning them. They will
be needed primarily to test and improve
the military industrial machine, to
undermine rising foreign economies,
and to shape public opinion. War will
become a vehicle for maintaining the
balance of economic and political forces;
the boundaries between it and peace
will likely be erased.

54

Variation on Milan Kundera.

GLOBALIZATION IS THE last failed hope
that, somewhere, there still exists a land
where one can escape and find happiness.

55

Variation on Isaac Bashevis Singer.

ONLY HE AND I will know how
I survived and even gained recognition
in an environment in which my people
and I were hated; only He and I will
know why they saw me as a prophet even
though they didn't understand me; only
He and I will know why I was loved by
a woman who risked her life to love me;
only He knows that one day I will stand
before him and admit that I believed in
Him too much to speak about it openly.

56

NON-JEWS USUALLY don't possess the
sensitivity or language to speak about
Jews, just as most men can't legitimately
speak about women. This leads to
extremes: either Jews are so admired
that they are barely considered a normal
people (one that includes the wise as well

as the villainous), or they are blamed for the lack of security in the Western world and for all of the sins of humanity. Is this thesis valid if we substitute Gentiles and Jews with men and women? In a sense. Seeking rights and recognition, women had to gain access to a world of culture and politics created by men, just as Jews had to find niches in a world dominated by Gentiles. In both cases only one side conformed and adapted — hence the asymmetry of sensibilities.

57

A PERSON IS born with neither freedom nor nation; life either brings these things together or pulls them apart.

58

PEOPLE ARE BORN only as the open possibility of freedom. But that does not make it right to enslave them.

59

IDENTITY IS THE fragile dream
of being like those with whom you
would like to identify, while
preserving your own uniqueness.

60

HATRED IS AN unbearable dichotomy
in which we imagine another's demise
while secretly hoping that he or she
will survive to deliver us from
meaninglessness.

61

REMBRANDT AND SHAKESPEARE
are geniuses of the same order.
They painted the story of the human
soul in every shade — from
wretchedness to greatness.

62

WHAT IS LITERARY criticism to its parent
discipline, modern philosophy? Not much
more than comments scribbled in the
margins of Shakespeare's tragedies
and Cervantes' *Don Quixote*.

63

THERE ARE TWO types of genius.
One is an author who creates an original
canon out of nothing or from some
fragment of his or her own experience.
The other is a pilfering magpie who
weaves all the interesting and sparkly
things of that era into new combinations.
It is enough to compare Dante
and Shakespeare, Bach and Mozart,
Masaccio and Filippino Lippi, Hals
and Johannes Verspronck, his Dutch
colleague and competitor.

64

SHAKESPEARE, CERVANTES, AND Mozart were brilliant pilfering magpies — they were like their contemporaries, only brighter. Masaccio, Rembrandt, Hals, and Vermeer were of a different order — they were unique and transcended their influences. The same is true of the Renaissance art geniuses who sprang out of nowhere, and of the self-invented soldiers of fortune in the professional armies of the era.

65

POLITICAL ABSOLUTISM AND fanaticism go hand in hand. Only an unbridled thirst for power and domination can make someone want to force others to be like him or her. That is like seeing other people as either an expression of one's will or as a threat to one's self.

66

WHY DO WE tend to be so intimate
and sensitive when bidding each other
goodnight? Is it because sleep is a bit like
death — a way of preparing, every night,
to eventually meet it? Is this not why we
are always happy to find, on waking, that
we have not yet been swallowed by
nothingness? This experience is described
perfectly by Sancho Panza, who ends his
monologue on the blessedness of sleep by
telling Don Quixote that only one thing
diminishes the joy of sleep, briefly
making us equals: it reminds us of death.

67

IF ONE IS unsure about who one is
and what to do with oneself, one is all
the more likely to have strong opinions
about others and what they should
do with themselves.

68

WHAT HAPPENS IF one does not have
a convincing narrative about oneself?
One is more likely to suffer from
narcissistic sensitivity and have difficulty
finding appropriate means of expression.

69

ANTI-SEMITISM IS the universal fear
that everything unrelated to Jews is
doomed to oblivion, helplessness, and
provincialism. It is the horror of grasping
one's insignificance, and the fantasy that
others are more powerful and influential
only by virtue of their origins or their
belonging to a more powerful group.

70

THE BEAUTY OF silence lies in the
knowledge that it can be interrupted at
any time. It is a word or a look directed
our way — something that can never
return, which will dissolve in an instant.

71

TOLERANCE IS THE understanding
that I was not born to edit other people's
lives and thoughts — that I must spend
my life editing myself.

72

THE ADULT'S SUPPOSED love of youth
often belies a fear of mature or
differently-minded competitors.

73

How NOT TO see others: look for
mirror images of ourselves in them,
as they do with us.

74

CANDIDE AND *DON* Quixote are deep
because they are at once amusing and sad.

75

A LONG KISS, and especially the gaze
that precedes it, are the best proof of the
insufficiency of individual existence.

76

WE THINK THAT happiness lies in the
fulfilment of great dreams and ambitions.
But in truth it lies in the details of
everyday life — everyday sounds, colours,
favourite objects, old books, music
albums, a cup of tea in the morning.
It is only when we lose these things that
we grasp their true worth.

77

AN INSTANT IS precious because it is
finite and unique. If it comes to set the
tone for one's entire life, it ceases to be
a fragment of time and becomes a clock
that meaninglessly and monotonously
marks the passage of time, and that
conveniently offers a precise sense
of one's approaching death.

78

HOW DOES AMBITION change us?
We no longer see what is happening
and risk misreading expressions and
faces, eyes and hands that could be
hinting at future, possibly life-altering
conversations. Wanting clarity and banal,
obvious truths, we fail to hear unfinished
sentences and innuendos, because
we no longer have time for nuance
and halftones. Loss of sight and hearing
are common side effects of the stellar
career; the cost of success is often
a changed personality and the
resulting loss of friends.

79

WHEN DO WE understand that
happiness lies in silence, pauses,
details, and the intervals between
taking trips and making plans? When
illness strikes or one loses a loved
one. Or when the implementation
of ambitious plans radically changes
one's lifestyle, forcing one to silently

endure an intolerable, inescapable
environment that gradually
erodes one's self.

80

CHILDREN OF HAPPY families are not
forced to grow up too quickly, to plunge
too early into the prose of life. The same
can be said about societies which respect
human freedom and spontaneity: their
young people are not brutally thrust
into the unpredictable adult world,
its breakneck socialization, or its ideas
about careers and success.

81

LET US NOT confuse the child's existential
wonder with the infantilism promoted
by a global mass culture that breeds
morally and psychologically immature
(but manipulative and insensitive)
consumers — socio-cultural teenagers
controlled by a system that shapes
their needs and imaginations, and
prevents them from ever growing up.

82

BY FORCING 18-year-olds who barely
know themselves to determine the course
of their lives by studying one thing
or another, are we not writing the scripts
of future tragedies? Can children be
happy if they begin to mimic adults early
on? Childhood and youth are the litmus
test of a society's freedom and humanity,
and both are radically limited by
totalitarian regimes. Neither the Nazis
nor the Bolsheviks allowed children
to simply be themselves, but trained
them to participate in the regime—to
join the party, the army, and the secret
police, to become technical workers
and informants.

83

WE REMEMBER AND talk about ideas we
respect, even if we don't believe in them.
While unlicensed hatred, or physical
or psychological torture, can never
be forgotten, inappropriate speaking,
nonsense, or pettiness are even more

deserving of contempt and disregard.
Disavowal is a classic form of punishment:
the phrase "I don't want to know you any
more" is an active and conscious form of
forgetting. If you can't stop talking about
something that should never have and
perhaps never will become the norm,
you are only extending its life.

84

A WRITER MUST read extensively not
in order to know what to write, but
to know what not to write. Similarly,
one must constantly listen carefully
to other people in order to know what
should never be said.

85

A YOUNG PERSON who thinks that he
or she knows about old age has the
charming naiveté of a man who thinks
he knows what it is to be a woman.
It is possible to see without knowing,
as it is to know without seeing.

86

LIKE SILENCE, CONSTANT joking is
a perfect mask — one that fits the wise
person as well as the fool.

87

THE EASE WITH which we remember
the crimes of others, in particular those
committed far away, usually masks
an unwillingness to recall our own
transgressions.

88

WE LEAF THROUGH a favourite book
much as we reflect on our own lives:
either by reading closely or by skipping
from one part to another. In the end,
it is important to do both.

89

A BOOK IS a testament to both the human
cycle of life and our resistance to
mortality. This duality is most enigmatic
when we are leafing through one
of our favourite texts.

90

DECLARED SCEPTICISM ABOUT a
possibility usually masks a secret fantasy
about its realization. I will never become
that which I dream of becoming,
but there's a chance someone might
hear that "never ..."

91

A SOCIETY'S DESIRE to physically
or quantitatively surpass another belies
its cultural depletion and fundamental
barbarity. It is an admission that all
they can do to outpace us is produce
more babies.

92

THE UNCHECKED GROWTH of
bureaucracy and the increasing
acceptance of its inevitability belie
a fundamental, almost medieval, lack
of faith in the individual — a blind
dependence on institutional control.

93

THE TWENTIETH CENTURY media
universe profoundly transformed the
public figure. In the eighteenth century,
public intellectuals lived their societies'
concerns, raising them to the level
of philosophical and political discourse.
But, while they saw private problems
in public terms and engaged private
persons with public concerns and
interests, they themselves avoided the
social noise of public life. It was once
considered a sign of good taste and
correct attitude to avoid the press.
A Victorian Englishwoman was expected

to appear in it only three times in her
life: on the very special occasions of
birth, marriage, and death. In our era,
to appear in the media a mere three
times would be equivalent to not
having existed at all.

94

IN VOLTAIRE'S TIMES public figures
had secretaries to help them avoid
excessive scrutiny and the cacophony
of public life. Today famous people have
press secretaries whose express role is to
engineer their employers' public profiles
by gradually revealing details of their
private lives — in small, homeopathic
doses, so as to steadily build the curiosity
and ardour of the masses.

95

Variation on Zygmunt Bauman.

POPULAR CULTURE AND the media have
transformed our common public life
into an arena for discussing the details
of celebrities' private problems.

96

WE FIND BEAUTY in landscapes which remind us of what we once were or what we might have been; nature is a projection of our souls and our memories.

97

IT IS BEAUTIFUL when something repeats itself unexpectedly, especially when it reminds us of our most intimate, indescribable experiences.

98

WICKEDNESS IS THE conscious decision to see and do everything in amoral terms — to appeal to standards in terms that negate them.

99

AUTHORITARIAN LOVE IS a foil for hatred.

100

SHORT-LIVED HATRED contains the secret hope that the object of one's obsession will open up a path to love and other forms of affection.

101

LONG-LIVED HATRED is a slow form of suicide. Just as a long gaze between lovers inevitably ends in a kiss, an enduring hatred always ends in one's own and one's enemy's destruction. It is a union in loathing, a shared kiss of death.

102

IN MIKHAIL LERMONTOV's short story "Taman," from the cycle *A Hero for Our Time*, Grigory Pechorin sees a blind boy and admits to himself that he has never trusted the disabled, suspecting that physical imperfections inevitably lead to defects of the soul. Although I reject this misanthropic idea, I would like to explore how it can be applied to close

family relations. While it is barbaric
to blame children for their parents' sins,
it would be foolish to ignore the powerful
human impulse to extend the past and
preserve family legends. In the best cases,
the offspring of criminals and traitors
devote their lives to denying their
parents, becoming miserable in the
process. In the worst, they try to relive
their parents' legendary lives, becoming
even unhappier caricatures.

103

WHILE COURAGE IS an extension of
curiosity about and acceptance of one's
own death, cowardice and brutality deny
death and reflect a lack of interest
in others. That is why, if cowardice
and guile are cruel, courage never is.

104

DECENCY IS A form of moral identification
with the self — it is the desire to be the
best that one can be, and the refusal
to accept mediocre alternatives.

105

IDEALISM IS REALISM about
the past or the future.

106

IN SMALL COUNTRIES, politicians
are doomed to the politics of freedom
and identity, because they never really
accede to the arenas of power.

107

PANDERING TO VILLAINS and the fear
of naming them are two sides of the
same coin——and a great source
of evil's strength.

108

THE RELATIONSHIP BETWEEN a nation's
power and its influence on a politician's
success is like the relationship between
a dictatorship's brutality and knowledge
of its crimes in the world. While power

naturally glorifies its heroes and victims,
fame usually eludes both a small
nation's leaders and the victims of their
anti-democratic policies.

109

WHY ARE LEFT-leaning Western
politicians generally more appealing
than their right-wing counterparts?
Is it not because, with its fear of
the future and idealization of canon,
the Right—and especially its most
conservative branches—represents
humanity's metaphysical and political
old age? And is not the Left an expression
of metaphysical and political youth?

110

A YOUNG CONSERVATIVE is a premature
misanthrope. An old socialist is
a late-blooming visionary. How are
they related? They both dislike the age
they are and the age they live in.

111

LOVE IS THE refusal to see oneself
as the only reality, and the transcendence
of fear and hatred.

112

WE LOVE ONLY those things whose
fragile and temporary nature we are
acutely aware of.

113

SHAME IS A primal ethical insight — that
I am never, and nowhere, entirely alone.

114

CONSCIENCE IS AN intuition — that
wherever two meet, a third
is always present.

115

TALENT IS THE ability to write tens
or hundreds of pages in the hope of
suddenly producing that one sentence
that will make it all worthwhile
(and easy to discard the rest).

116

JUST AS CONTEMPORARY Egypt has
nothing to do with ancient Egyptian
civilization, or Iran's theocratic Shiite
Muslim regime with the majestic
and tolerant world of the Persian
Zoroastrians, so today's Greece is
but a political descendant of Byzantium.
The physical ruins of its glorious
predecessor have nothing to do with
the present — they could just as easily
be located in another country.

117

CONTEMPORARY FLEMISH AND Dutch
faces often bear strong resemblances to
those in portraits by Rubens, van Dyck,
and Hals. The freedom and equality
resulting from these countries'
early adoption of modern ideas allowed
greater numbers of people to have
a sense of individual dignity.
The result — more portraits,
and a stronger feeling for the genre.

118

TODAY'S ITALIAN CINEMATOGRAPHER
is a descendant of the great painters.
Pier Paolo Pasolini's *Decameron* continues
the work of the great Renaissance
masters, in particular Masaccio
and Giotto (whose student is played
by Pasolini in the film). Similarly, Andrei
Tarkovsky's *Andrei Rublev* revives
the works of Theophanes the Greek,
Rublev, and Russian iconography.

119

Variation on Eric Fromm.

THE SADISTIC NEED to torture another
living being is caused by solitude,
isolation, and insecurity: I am no longer
alone because another suffers with me,
so the emptiness, meaninglessness,
and psychological hell that torture
me temporarily subside.

120

THE NATIONALIST CAN usually
acknowledge truths about his or her
nation's present, but refuses to speak
unpleasant truths about its past.
The adherent of *realpolitik* is not afraid
of the past, but speaks very carefully,
if at all, about the present.
The chauvinistic imperialist denies
unpleasant truths about the past
and the present with equal vigour.

121

CAN POLITICIANS SPEAK freely,
unhindered by thoughts about whether
or not they will appeal to the public?
They can, if they represent great
countries. Politicians from small
countries must win the favour of as many
people, and countries, as possible.
The same applies to representatives
of small and large political parties.

122

POWER AND FAITH are twin
brothers — the tension between them
engenders freedom. Conversely, a lack
of connection between them can deform
the life of a society. While power without
faith produces a cynical political
environment, faith without power can
easily result in abstract humanism
or even a sectarian denial of concrete
responsibility for humanity. On the other
hand, the union of power and faith
engenders absolutism and fanaticism. That

is why, to this day, no one has conceived
of a better way to guarantee freedom than
the tension between faith and power.

123

DOES AUTHORITY UNRECOGNIZABLY
deform a person, or does it simply
eliminate the feelings of unease that
previously masked their most dangerous
traits? Perhaps it simply accelerates
or radicalizes those comic, rather than
tragic, characteristics that would have
surfaced sooner or later. Power and
authority often confuse forms
and genres — combining comedy
and tragedy, epic and farce.

124

TWO SOLITUDES DO not beget a wholeness.

125

ENVY RESULTS FROM self-hatred and
the secret longing to find happiness in the

appropriation of someone else's identity or biography. Envy never has a memory of its own existence and registers only other people's stories. Nor does it have plans for the future, because it imagines that happiness lies in another's destiny — as long as it is stolen and preserved in time. *Amor fati* is foreign to it.

126

ELOQUENCE ON THE occasion of another person's misfortune comes from a euphoric mixture of pain and the relief that, for now, one has been spared.

127

"NOBODY" IS NOT someone who is unknown, but someone who doesn't want to know anything — not someone who is unimportant, but someone for whom nothing is important.

128

Variations on Renaissance philosophy.

EMPTINESS THAT IS the deliberate
product of knowledge is falsehood
and self-deception; emptiness that arises
from ignorance is a precondition for
thought and doubt; emptiness that is
born of ignorance is folly.

129

Three variations on the
theme of power.

MICHEL FOUCAULT. POWER lies in
the ability to see everything, while
remaining unseen oneself. Growing
to believe that he or she is continually
observed, the object of observation
is gradually disempowered.

ZYGMUNT BAUMAN. IN our contemporary, liquid modernity, power is manifested in the ability to strike while remaining unseen and inaccessible; in a more solid, or earlier, modernity, power was manifested through the occupation of foreign territories — by proclaiming their defeat to the whole world and modifying, or even completely rewriting, their histories.

DANIEL J. BOORSTIN. Power is the ability to be seen to the degree that you want — neither more nor less — and to be seen as you want to be, not how others decide to see you. Then you are known for your fame and seen for your visibility.

130

Variations on world chess champion Boris Spassky's thoughts about Estonian grandmaster Paul Keres.

ONLY THOSE WHO are obsessed with victory — who are able to forget

themselves and others — can become
champions. Victory evades the generous,
aristocratic, classically well-mannered
person; a noble-hearted, philosophical
competitor without killer instinct always
undermines his or her own chances
of winning. (Paul Keres beat all
of the world's champions and had five
opportunities to become one himself,
but never did.)

131

Two variations on Machiavellian
and Shakespearean themes.

VARIATION I. FALSEHOOD is a highly
developed political method, not some
kind of unpleasant deviation from the
norm. The West and Russia illustrate
this perfectly. I know that they are lying,
and they know that I know that they are
lying. The transparency of lying makes
it a convenient political tool. If I lie,
you will allow me to operate unmasked,
because you too want to be free to
prevaricate. While lying accelerates

action, truth and conscience (the search
for truth, rather than power) force
us to question, verify, and analyze.
Truth slows us down and saps our energy
(just as, according to the murderer in
Richard III, conscience makes us cowards;
or, as Romeo said, love makes us
feminine and indecisive). Lying,
on the other hand, stimulates action
and productivity. That is why Hamlet
forsakes the throne of Denmark the
moment that his plan of action becomes
vague and his desire to understand
his traitorous mother's villainy
overwhelms his desire for revenge.

VARIATION II. LYING is an indispensable
political method — not some unsavoury
deviation from the norm. It is
predictable, which makes it a very
convenient tool in politics. If I lie,
you will allow me to continue to
operate unmasked, because you too
want to be unconstrained in your
lying — unhindered by unpleasant
comments and inconvenient facts.
Lying accelerates action, while truth

requires doubt and careful analysis.
Truth hinders us and robs us of precious
time and energy, while telling falsehoods
promotes action and productivity.
In the world of efficient action,
truth is an annoying obstacle.

132

THE HEIGHT OF political virtuosity is
the ability to insert your own text about
yourself into someone else's mouth — to
convince them that they are expressing
their own heartfelt views.

133

WHEN IS POWER one with language?
When one can impose one's own
words on whom, about what,
and whenever one wants.

134

AN ATHLETIC OR political champion
cannot be too philosophical or too
civilized. While it is philosophical

to play honourably and lose graciously,
the instinct to compete and conquer
is always marked by an element of
barbarity — it combines the brutality
of the child and the rage of the barbarian.
Champions must accept that their
victories result from a combination of
brutality and skill, barbarity and civility.

135

Only someone who can live without
authority is morally worthy of it.

136

Rhetorical excess or deathly
silence — these are two fragile and barely
discernible bulwarks between the
superfluity and absence of thought.

137

How does the demagogue of a
totalitarian regime compare to his
or her counterpart in a democracy?
The former generally raves abroad but

is discreet at home (in both cases to avoid losing his or her head), while the latter suffers silently abroad but comes to life on home soil. Some of these characters are stunningly similar — the eloquent and impudent leaders of countries like Russia, Iran, and Sri Lanka, who brazenly defend their regimes to the West in order to save their own skins.

138

FANATICISM IS HATRED of those who don't identify with your beliefs and loyalties — who threaten your conviction that your own doctrine is universal.

139

Discreet fascism, or variations on Sergei Kovalev.

WESTERN EUROPEANS' NAIVETÉ about Russia is a convenient shield relieving them of conscience and responsibility. Could they not see what was happening in 1937, when Lion Feuchtwanger described Russia as a wonderful and progressive land, and Stalin as a great anti-fascist? But naiveté is just a mask — they understood everything then and they do now. They simply learned to live with a foreign fascism, even while refusing to tolerate their own; this is why the anti-fascist Feuchtwanger could be so supportive of the "anti-fascist" Stalin.

.

140

Variation on Russian human rights advocate Stanislav Dmitryevsky.

THE WEST'S POSITION on Russia: "I know that they are lying, and they know that I know."

141

Cultural-philosophical variations on Portugal.

THE PORTUGUESE NOTION of *Saudade* is a fusion of messianic melancholy, nostalgia, and expectation. It is from

this melancholy, and from the longing
for King Sebastian (who disappeared
mysteriously in Morocco in 1578)
that *fado* — a Portuguese music style
expressing sadness and longing — emerged
in the early nineteenth century. In 1580,
as Portugal entered a union with Spain
and lost its independence, the poet Luís
de Camões proclaimed that he would die
not alone but with his entire nation.
Waiting for Sebastian (in Portugal
this phenomenon is referred to as
"sebastianism") can also be associated
with salazarism, or the waiting for
saviours in the twentieth century.
Saudade's three main motifs are related
to the powerful experiences it reveals:
waiting at a port for sailors or relatives;
university students' melancholy songs
about the homes they left; and
anticipation of the king's return and
nostalgia for a lost empire. *Saudade*
is also related to the search for signs
of Portuguese influence in the
world — hence Fernando Pessoa's
thought that his homeland
is the Portuguese language.

142

Variation on Russian humorist
Arkady Arkanov.

A FREE PERSON is one who has the
strength to survive a friend's success.

143

ERUDITION IS NOT the parroting of
the words and opinions of others, but
the development of a personal language
for describing universal phenomena.

144

HAPPINESS LIES NOT in financial
or political power, but in finding
an intelligent relationship to power — in
reconciling one's limitations
with its different forms.

145

IN ART ONE is right (or successful)
when one can be silent, because one's

works speak for themselves. In
scholarship one is right when one's lips
speak logical and verifiable arguments.
In politics, power is right — or, rather,
majority rule (we are right because we
are greater in number); or else force,
when it makes us see that it is right.

146

WHEN PEOPLE GAIN wealth, fame,
and power too early in life, their
characters may be distorted rather
than developing normally. If these
things come too late, they do not
bring happiness, but can make the same
individuals grotesque and repulsive
to those who surround them.

147

ACCORDING TO ISAAC Bashevis Singer,
events are often wiser than people.
This is true, unless we are able
to recognize their significance. For how
many opportunities — how many wistful
looks, or people eager for our

response—do we fail to recognize?
Many! They pass by and disappear just
as we are dreaming about meeting them.

148

Three variations on the theme
of provincialism.

I. PROVINCIALISM IS the lack of language
and criteria for evaluating yourself and
your environment. It is an inability to
assess your own worth—a desperate
plea for others to identify and assess you.

II. PROVINCIALISM IS the inability to
believe that life is happening exactly
where you are—the fear that it will
happen there where you are not.

III. PROVINCIALISM IS the inability
to believe that you are responsible for
yourself and the world—the conviction
that someone else, somewhere else,
is responsible.

149

Variations on Oscar Wilde.

PHYSICAL BEAUTY IS the unselfconscious wisdom of a body that has been perfectly formed by nature. It is an emotional wisdom that does not understand itself, that is dispersed in the body, and therefore cannot see that body as its opposite. Physical beauty is a fragile and finite form of perfection — it moves us precisely because it masks the reality of death and ending. It is a temporary perfection that has chosen the body and not the soul.

150

GREAT ART DISSOLVES our illusions about the importance and truth of the present.

151

MASTERPIECES CAUSE REALITY to penetrate us; mediocre works force us to penetrate and distort reality.

152

CORRESPONDENCE WITH PEOPLE whom
we no longer expect to see is a desperate
attempt to prevent a rapidly dissolving
image of the past from receding from us.

153

Faith + knowledge = wisdom.
Faith − knowledge = ignorance.
Knowledge − faith = despair.
Faith + hope = love.
Faith − hope = hatred.
Knowledge + hope = idealism.
Knowledge − hope = cynicism.

154

WISDOM HAS NO age and no allegiances.

155

IN LOVE AND friendship
we ignore age and ancestry.

156

EVERY FORM OF evil has its own theory
and justifying ethics. Conformism is based
on the belief (and the tolerance of small
and large betrayals that come with it) in
a power that supposedly shapes us, and
which is attributed to each new person
we meet and each new life experience
that performs us. Conformists reject
the idea that they are responsible for, and
participate in, shaping the world — they
believe that the world is responsible
for them and creates them. Conformism
is unconditionally recognized power
raised to the level of pedagogy or public
faith. It differs fundamentally from
respect in that authentic respect never
abandons its object, even while
recognizing its errors and limitations.
Conformism, on the other hand, will
instantly transfer its loyalty to a new
object if circumstances require it,
gaining new strength from
its power and prestige.

157

EVERY EPOCH HAS its own designated
place, setting, and justifying mythologies.

158

C'EST FACILE, OR a Bruges étude.
I look long and closely at a favourite
painting — Hans Memling's *Portrait
of a Young Woman (Sibylla Sambetha)*
(1480). As I contemplate the veil
covering her face, it occurs to me that
the secret of beauty lies in the ability
to achieve lightness during an era heavy
with wars and disasters. A thought
about lightness comes to me in French:
c'est facile (it's easy). And a sudden
association — Mozart's wonderfully light
and beautiful *Sonata facile* (ital.). I leave
the Hans Memling Museum and walk
toward the Groeninge Museum, and
within ten minutes I can make out the
notes of Wolfgang Amadeus Mozart's
sonata — the very end of the first part.
A miracle? *C'est facile.*

159

SPEAKING THE TRUTH can sometimes take the form of humiliation and revenge.

160

PHYSICAL BEAUTY RESULTS when the nobility of the body temporarily surpasses that of the soul.

161

Variation on Milan Kundera.

WHEN OUR MEMORIES die, so do we.

162

HISTORICAL GREATNESS IS the result of a bygone politics losing its power and being transformed into culture and imagination.

163

WE ARE DISTURBED by dreams because
they displace reality and leave us unsure
of whether or not we are happy or safe.

164

WHAT IS ONE's homeland? The place
where one becomes a parent, or where
a parent was killed?

165

LIFE ACCORDING TO the Right: A feeling
of having roots, often without even
knowing what they are and whether they
actually lie there where one thinks.
Or, the determination to interrupt
the dynamically changing reality where
those roots must be located.

Life according to the Left: The rejection
of all roots and the search for oneself in
one's own, and the world's, changing

nature. Or in a radical self-negation which
ends in a fanatical move to the Right.

Two faces of modernity.

166

THE RIGHT IS the political equivalent
of the existential relation to the mother,
the Left — an extension of the
fundamental relationship to the father.

167

A FRIEND IS someone with whom one
does not have to justify one's existence.

168

A FRIEND IS someone for whom
one's success does not become
one's greatest weakness.

169

The Sabbath Elevator

JUNE 11, 2010. Jerusalem, Israel.
A hotel. The nineteenth floor. Four
elevators. A computer system which
one merely speaks to. I am standing near
the doors to elevators C and D with
a young man who looks American.
The elevator doesn't come. In a thick
American accent the young man begins
to castigate the elevator and complain
violently to me. Quietly suggesting
that the system is probably overwhelmed,
I let him squeeze desperately into the
packed C elevator that finally arrives,
and move towards the doors for A and B.
When a B elevator arrives, I enter it,
joining a black-clad Orthodox Jew.
The elevator begins to descend slowly,
but only two floors at a time. When
it stops it beeps repeatedly, lets in new
passengers, beeps again and goes
down two more floors.

"It's a Sabbath elevator," says my smiling
fellow traveller. "On the Sabbath we

can't actively ask it to come, so it goes
up and down on its own, two floors
at a time. It's strange and inconvenient,
but quite amusing."

Smiling myself, I reply that this
suits me perfectly well.

"You are sure that you did not make
a mistake? Perhaps you should have taken
another one?" my new acquaintance
persists, trying to console me.

"No," I reply. "I really do find
this pleasant and interesting."

The other passengers are quiet. They
are calm and smiling, very different
from the ones in the C and D elevators.
Both types of elevators are completely
computerized — the latest in technical
sophistication. Only one is for the
non-religious, the other for believers.

Two modernities in two types of
elevator. Universal modernity and
Sabbath modernity — in the universal
elevators and the Sabbath elevators.

170

Repatriation of a Lithuanian Jew

LITHUANIA. A MAN. The parents'
apartment. The brother. The wife.
The son. Israel. The wife and son stay
there. They return. The business fails.
Divorce. The son returns. The wife
returns. The father dies. A grandson
is born. The mother dies. The parents'
apartment. An empty apartment.
The apartment is for sale. The man
and the cat. Lithuania.

171

Le temps passe vite. Il faut profiter de la vie, n'est-ce pas?

*LE TEMPS PASSE vite. Il faut profiter de la
vie, n'est-ce pas?* Time passes quickly, so
shouldn't one make the most of life?
These are the words of a brilliant thinker
whom I am lucky to count as a friend.
But how do you celebrate life when one
day you wake up old, even if you know
what it is to be young — even better than

young people? There is no difference
between old age and youth, except that
now the young faces are laughing at you.
The world is the same at it always was,
and you, who finally understand
everything and are ready to experience
each day more profoundly than before,
will no longer have time to do that.

172

In Alexandre Dumas' footsteps

IN ONE OF Alexandre Dumas' famous
novels, what does the Sun King's
controller general of finances (in today's
terms, his minister of finance), Jean
Baptiste Colbert, tell the king from
his deathbed? He gives the king
a very valuable piece of advice: don't
ever appoint another controller
general of finances.

And what advice can an intellectual,
who became involved in and is already
withdrawing from politics, give to a
young person? Don't be friends with
politicians. Don't ever seek emotional

intimacy with them. If you do, they will turn you into a version of themselves.

173

A POLITICIAN'S OLD and close friends can only interact sincerely with that person after he or she has been defeated. In the case of victory, friends are quickly replaced by people who forge professional bonds only with winners.

174

CONSPIRACY THEORY IS the illusion that someone in the world is so interested in you that they long for your demise and will do everything to destroy you.

175

TO RECEIVE AWARDS and honours on an important anniversary is a mute form of appreciation which tells you that someone is grateful that you have less time to live, and that your creative powers are waning.

176

Everyday life in the global village

I DON'T WANT to buy headphones in
Lithuania, because they are usually
cheaper and of better quality in the US.
But I don't have time to purchase any in
Washington, so I decide to go into a shop
at Copenhagen Airport. A young salesman
shows me a set that I've never seen before,
and whose quality surpasses any that I have
ever tried. Seeing my ticket, the young
man asks if I am from Lithuania. I reply
that I am. "I am Lithuanian too," he tells
me with a friendly smile. In quite good
Lithuanian, he quickly explains that he is
an American Lithuanian, currently living
in Malmö and working in Copenhagen.
"My brother speaks Lithuanian better
than me, because he has lived there," Eric
Vytautas Ž. tells me warmly. I only smile,
thinking about my new headphones, which
I had not wanted to buy in Lithuania.
And about how Lithuanian globalization
caught up with me in Copenhagen.
The headphones are perfect. German.

177

Fear those who fear nothing,
not even themselves, and doubt
the majority, which never doubts
its righteousness.

178

Be fearful of the fearless
and doubtful of the undoubting.

179

All idealists are similar in
their goals; they only differ in their
methods. Some do not recognize any
compromise and turn to fanaticism.
Others accept compromise up
to a certain point, where their
fundamental principles begin.
A third group is open to compromise
on all issues and in all situations;
they become professional politicians
or bureaucrats, leaving their past
idealism for their memoirs.

180

VILLAINY DOES NOT usually lie in our
goals, but in our means of pursuing them.

181

EVERY COUNTRY'S MODERN consumer
paradise is the same; every country's
modern hell of emotional insecurity
is different.

182

À l'amour

I AM WAITING for the elevator on the
tenth floor of the European Parliament.
A friendly cleaning woman whom
I recognize is chatting with another
building employee, when the man
sneezes violently. And again, and then
several times more, each time more
briskly. In my mind I say "God bless you,"
because this is how one expresses one's
best wishes to someone in English, when

they are at risk of expelling their soul.
The cleaning woman smiles at him and
says, "À l'amour." To love. In Lithuanian,
one would wish someone good health.
In the same situation Americans make
reference to a person's vulnerability
and need for grace. The French genius
for language finds a different solution.
Everything comes back to love — our
lack or longing for it.

The next day, as I go to my office
on the same tenth floor, I remember
this episode. Smiling to myself, I see
the same man pass me by. In my thoughts
I long to say to him, "À l'amour."
But he is not sneezing.

183

Ars longa, vita brevis

IN STRASBOURG I get into a European
Parliament vehicle. Beautiful classical
music is playing. It makes me happy to
think that in this city even chauffeurs
appreciate real art and high culture.

Suddenly the chauffeur turns off the
classical music. It makes me sad that he
might think that because I am a politician
I probably don't like classical music.
Am I to start explaining to him that I am
a different kind of politician — not really
a politician, not only a politician?

We are an uncultured lot, we
europarliamentarians. So what if the
station has been turned off and the music
is no longer playing; I am being driven
along in silence, and my life will go on.
The driver is not mistaken. He doesn't
even know that this episode, which
perhaps meant nothing to him, has
reminded me of a simple truth:
Ars longa, vita brevis.

184

CAN INTELLIGENT THOUGHTS and
intelligent actions be reconciled?
Can a thought remain intelligent once
it begins to be translated into action?
Does action not, in and of itself, discredit
thought? Can we remain intelligent only

by being indecisive and politically weak?
Is it possible to work simultaneously
in these two spheres without deforming
thought and paralyzing action?
Hamlet's dilemma. Its origins lie in the
Renaissance idea of the brave mind
(*la mente audace*). Hamlet simply arrests
the development of the intelligent
Machiavellian animal within his soul — at
the cost of friendship and his own life.

185

EVERY BOOK IS a form of quiet
gratitude — to the ideas, people,
and encounters that formed it.

186

Two variations on Fran Lebowitz.

MIDDLE AGE IS the time when it is no
longer the magic of sex, but that of food,
that one is beginning to discover.
The mid-life crisis is the final resistance
to this transition.

HAPPINESS IS A feeling. Just like a feeling
for the form of history or a work of art.
Objectively it does not exist. Happiness
does not exist as objects and people do.
It can only be experienced. That is why
it is fundamentally wrong to try to see
it as a human norm or criterion, and but
a fantasy wrought by our pragmatic
utilitarian modernity.

187

LET US NOT make fun of those who enter
the sphere of politics. It is no longer
acceptable to joke — whether in a
stylized or foolish way — about women
when they become actors in the drama
of politics and enter the global field and
discourse of power. As various plants
and animals also enter and become
established in this field, symbolic
transferences should gradually recede,
beginning with the classical metaphors:
there will be no more room for young
maidens as white as swans, just as it will
become impossible to speak of a man

being as predatory as a wolf, because they will all be participants in the distribution of political sensibilities. Preservation of the swan and the wolf will require the rejection of pre-political magic and poetry as dangerous fictions. The same will apply to colour and race. The whole world is politics. As a result we have been freed from the stereotypes and nonsense of our prior experience. But we will also lose humour, which was born of none other than stereotype — from safe nonsense in an unsafe world — and powerlessness. Politics is about empowerment, which is why it cannot tolerate weakness. The brilliant humour of the Jews is a perfect example of existence on the other side of the field of power. The political humour of our times, with its safe flirtation with power, is politics in its truest form. It is no longer anti-structure or linguistic carnival, but a light and breezy adjustment to the structure and field of power. It is also a warning: Ladies and gentlemen, you are not the only ones here. Share or you will perish.

188

WHO CAN TELL jokes safely? A fool or
a simpleton — someone who is beyond
power hierarchies. In other words,
someone not of this world. The humour
of the person-outside-the-field-of-power
is authentic, because it is safe not to laugh
at it. When someone of higher stature
makes a joke, even a very weak one,
it is dangerous not to laugh. It is
forbidden. Mandatory.

189

THE CONTRADICTORY NATURE of
humour. We joke to reinforce our
freedom and independence, but also
out of powerlessness. But self-inflicted
weakness is sometimes liberating,
and that is perhaps the true power of
humour. Humour can also be imitated
mechanically — not only out of the desire
to appear stronger, but when, in
moments of danger, one dons a mask,
erasing one's dangerous identity or
individuality for the sake of personal

safety. Like compulsive smiling,
it is a sign of our contemporary
insecurity and unsafety.

190

WITH SOME AUTHORS, every new
book connotes a widely-cited master
yet again trying on new livery.

191

ACADEMICS ARE PAID for what they say.
Politicians and diplomats — for what
they do not say.

192

THE ESSENCE OF civilized discourse lies
not in what we discuss, but in what we
conceal. Not in what we say, but in what
we withhold from each other in order to
save ourselves and others from emotional
hell — from intercourse as perpetual
analysis or the rewriting of our own
and other people's life stories.

193

CIVILITY — THE FUSION of sociable and polite behaviour — requires us to limit our use of words and topics. It is letting, for the sake of easy and unfettered discourse, another speak in his or her language rather than imposing our own.

194

IT IS UNETHICAL to remain silent when another is trying to speak, or to speak incessantly when another wishes to be silent.

195

STATISTICS ARE MORE important than a real person's life, and a country's size and political power are by far more important than one of its inhabitants, even if that person speaks in the name of all humanity. It's nothing personal — just business.

196

HAPPINESS IS BORN of longing — for
longed-for repetition, especially of
a precious moment, or for return
to a longed-for place.

197

ANTHONY VAN DYCK may have died
before reaching old age, but he grasped
its secret. An old person, like an old
object, has become an individual — a
vessel of existence and history.

198

WHY DO WE become adults? To answer
the questions we asked in childhood.
Our adult lives are revisions to the child's
blueprints of life and the world.

199

DEATH PRESENTS ITSELF like a dream.
It comes like an invitation to enter
through the gates of the *città dolente*
of Ingmar Bergman's and Luis Buñuel's

films. In Federico Fellini's films, death is
not the city of the dead, but an invitation
to join one's parents. Just as we joined
them when we were born.

200

THERE IS ONLY one way for parents and
children who torture each other to find
a way out of their emotional hell — they
must simply change places.

201

Variation on Carl Schmitt.

POLITICS IS EVERYONE at war with
everyone else; the winners are those who
are first to recognize, or turn someone
else into, their common enemy.

202

THERE IS NOTHING more meaningless
than becoming involved in another
generation's war. This was the futility
of Tybalt's life and death.

203

THE PARADOX OF getting older:
the better you understand yourself as
the years go by, the less you will be able
to grasp what you long for and hope
that life will give you.

204

FRIENDSHIP IS A-historical. It makes
no difference when two people become
close friends. Friendship is measured
not in years, but in experiences. Its secret
lies in the mysterious knowledge that
you need each other.

205

European multilingualism

STRASBOURG CATHEDRAL. CROWDS
of tourists. The mid-day sun.
A woman runs up to me and asks
frantically, "*Entschuldigung*, where is
kostiol?" Understanding that the Russian

term following words in two European
Union languages refers to her desire
to see Strasbourg Cathedral, I tell her,
in Russian, that she is standing next to it,
and direct her to the entrance. Relieved,
she shouts to her travelling companions:
"You see, people in Strasbourg
even speak Russian!"

Note: *Entschuldigung* (German)—
Excuse me. *Kostiol* (Russian)—church.

206

Political eyes

THEY ARE EYES that see nothing.
That don't see you. Then suddenly,
one day, they light up, as though you
were a beloved old friend. They see
you. During an important discussion
they practically devour you. Afterwards,
they gently see you off. And once
again they are eyes that see nothing.
As before, eyes that do not
notice you. A politician's eyes.

207

IN DEATH A friend extended my
life — by redrafting the cartography
of my thoughts and becoming the subject
of my new book.

208

A FRIEND'S DEATH becomes a subject
that rescues my floundering new book.

209

WHY IS IT sometimes unappealing
to return to the city in which you
were born, raised, and became
an adult? Because you knew too
much about the people alongside
whom you grew and changed.
Resisting your evolution, they see
only one slice of the past and the final
result. And they know that you know
that they know this.

210

LIFE HAS NO logic. But it can be
meaningful to live it for someone
else — for a student or for someone
who loves you.

211

JOHN STUART MILL once said: "I am
not saying that all conservatives are
fools. I am only saying that all fools
are conservatives." One could also say:
"I am not saying that all anti-Semites
are fools. I am only saying that all
fools are anti-Semites."

212

THE KAUNAS JAZZ Festival. The jazz
trumpet virtuoso Arturo Sandoval
addresses an enthusiastic crowd: "Who
among you know of the great trumpet
player Timofei Dokshizer, who recently

died in Vilnius?" (Dokshizer was a
legendary Russian trumpeter who lived
in Lithuania, and who was known from
childhood on for his unforgettable
performance of the Neapolitan Dance
in Tchaikovsky's *Swan Lake*.) The deathly
silence was understandable, for no one
came to Sandoval's concert to discover
unknown locals. "Timofei Dokshizer was
an exceptional trumpeter and teacher.
I dedicate this composition to him.
Is his wife in the hall?" A small, modest
woman — Dokshizer's widow — stands
up. "Thank you," says Sandoval.

Memory comes from somewhere else.
Memory comes from the Other. We only
think that we preserve the memory
of a place, when in truth it comes from
elsewhere to preserve us. We need
the sensation of being created, founded,
and proclaimed to the world, when in
fact it is others who bear witness about
us to the world. The memory that saves

us from non-being comes from
elsewhere. Memory does not live here.
Memory lives elsewhere.

213

Three variations on Ludwig Wittgenstein's
philosophical diaries.

A JEW IS not a person of flesh and blood,
but a trajectory of consciousness and a
longing of the soul — an attempt to
defeat power through language and art.

TO BE A Jew is to attempt to name
the unnameable, to verbalize what
can't be verbalized, and to speak about
that which elicits shame, laughter,
mockery, or silence.

A JEW IS an obsession with language.
Not with survival through language,
but with death in language — in every
hymn, song, prayer, and joke.

214

Variation on Milan Kundera.

SEX IS A lament by two bodies about
the short and ephemeral nature of
wholeness. And about the fact that,
when it is over, solitude, longing,
and existential frustration will
once again reassert themselves.

215

SEX IS ABOUT learning to not fear death,
to greet it joyfully. Because the act of
love is a small death — a white maiden
who kisses us and departs safely, knowing
that we were firmly spoken for long ago.

About The Book

To entail, scan and embrace more knowledge of "what is" and "what ought to be done" in fewer words — to make a statement as short, concise, terse and pithy as possible while rendering the sights it opens as vast as possible — is the principal intention of the practitioners of the difficult art of the aphorism. Many writers have tried it, few have succeeded. A successful aphorism, true to its mission, allows a small step to go a long, perhaps an infinitely long, way. But as knowledge needed to find one's way in our increasingly crowded and complex world grows at a mind-boggling pace, so do the difficulties on the road to success. In our liquid-modern times horizons tend to break up or dissolve as soon as they are drawn. It is this unprecedented quality of our condition that Leonidas Donskis attempts to grasp and convey by resurrecting the badly missed and badly needed art of the aphorism, injecting into it a new impetus, a perfect match to the vertiginous pace of our life, and bringing that art up to the gravity and grandiosity of the challenge we confront. We should all be grateful to him for this exquisitely harrowing task he has performed ...

— ZYGMUNT BAUMAN
(sociologist and philosopher,
Professor Emeritus of Sociology,
University of Leeds)

About The Author

———◆◆◆———

Elected a member of the European Parliament in 2009, Leonidas Donskis is a philosopher, political theorist, historian of ideas, social analyst, and political commentator. As a public figure in Lithuania, he also acts as a defender of human rights and civil liberties. Born on August 13, 1962, in Klaipeda, Lithuania, Donskis received his first doctorate in philosophy from the University of Vilnius, and later earned his second doctorate in social and moral philosophy from the University of Helsinki, Finland. His scholarly interests lie in philosophy of history, philosophy of culture, philosophy of literature, philosophy of the social sciences, civilization theory, political theory, history of ideas, and studies in Central and East European thought.

Donskis is the author or editor of thirty four books, fifteen of them in English. He is co-author (with Zygmunt Bauman) of *Moral Blindness: The Loss of Sensitivity in Liquid Modernity* (Cambridge, England: Polity, 2013) and author of *Modernity in Crisis: A Dialogue on the Culture of Belonging* (New York: Palgrave Macmillan, 2011), *Troubled Identity and the Modern World* (New York: Palgrave Macmillan, 2009), *Power and Imagination: Studies in Politics and Literature* (New York: Peter Lang, 2008), *Loyalty, Dissent, and Betrayal: Modern Lithuania and East-Central European Moral Imagination* (Amsterdam: Rodopi, 2005), *Forms of Hatred: The Troubled Imagination in Modern Philosophy and Literature* (Amsterdam: Rodopi, 2003; VIBS-Value Inquiry Book Series Nomination for the 2003 Best Book in Social Philosophy in North America; VIBS 2003 Best Book Award), *Identity and Freedom: Mapping Nationalism and Social Criticism in Twentieth-Century Lithuania* (London: Routledge, 2002), and *The End of Ideology and Utopia? Moral Imagination and Cultural*

Criticism in the Twentieth Century (New York: Peter Lang, 2000).

Donskis' works originally written in Lithuanian and English have been translated into Danish, Estonian, Finnish, German, Hungarian, Italian, Polish, Portuguese, Romanian, Russian, Swedish, and Ukrainian.

From 2005 to 2009, he served as a Member of the Standing Committee for the Humanities (SCH) in the European Science Foundation (ESF). On 7 June 2009, Donskis was elected a Member of the European Parliament.

In 2004, Donskis was awarded by the European Commission the title of the Ambassador for Tolerance and Diversity in Lithuania. In 2008, Donskis received from Queen Beatrix of The Netherlands the Orange-Nassau Order Commander's Cross. In 2011, he has received an honorary degree (Honorary Degree of Doctor of Letters) from the University of Bradford, the UK.

About The Translator

Karla Gruodis has lived and worked in both Canada and Lithuania and is currently a member of the Department of English at Dawson College in Montreal. Former editor of *The Lithuanian Review*, and editor/author of *Feminizmo ekskursai* (Pradai, 1995), she specializes in the translation and editing of scholarly writing, and is a practicing artist.

Printed in March 2013
by Gauvin Press,
Gatineau, Québec